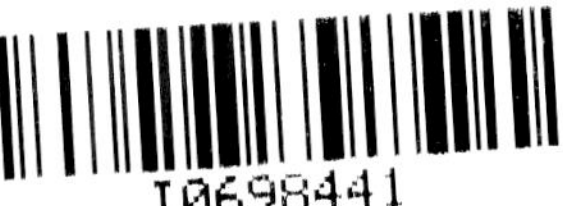

I am grateful to God for everything! And I believe that the meaning of life is to make sense of other lives.

Tânia Moreira
2024

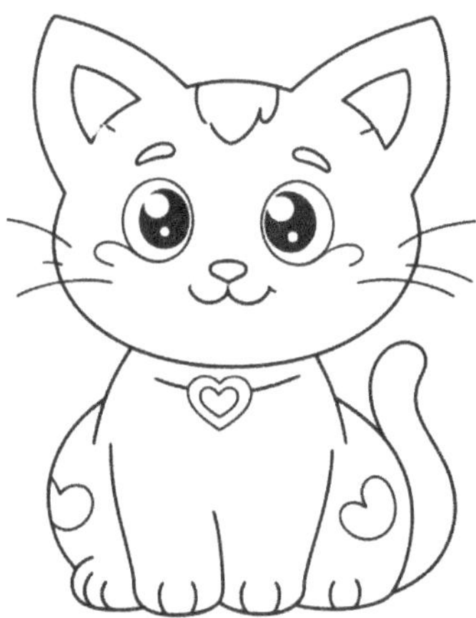
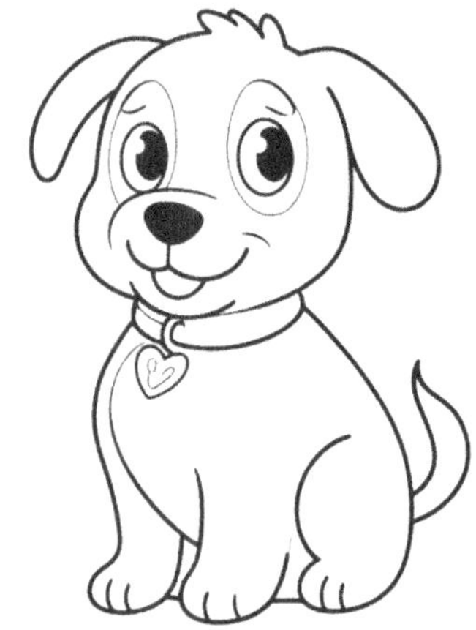

This Book Belongs to:

____

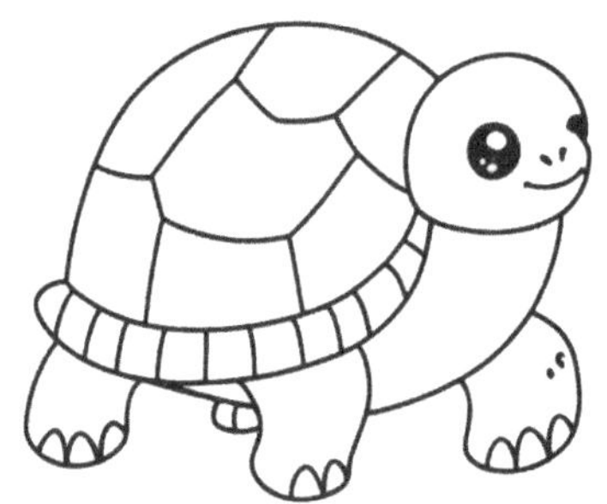
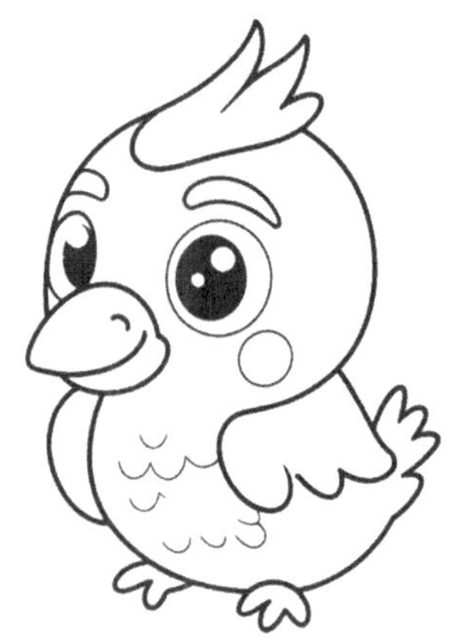

Test Color Page

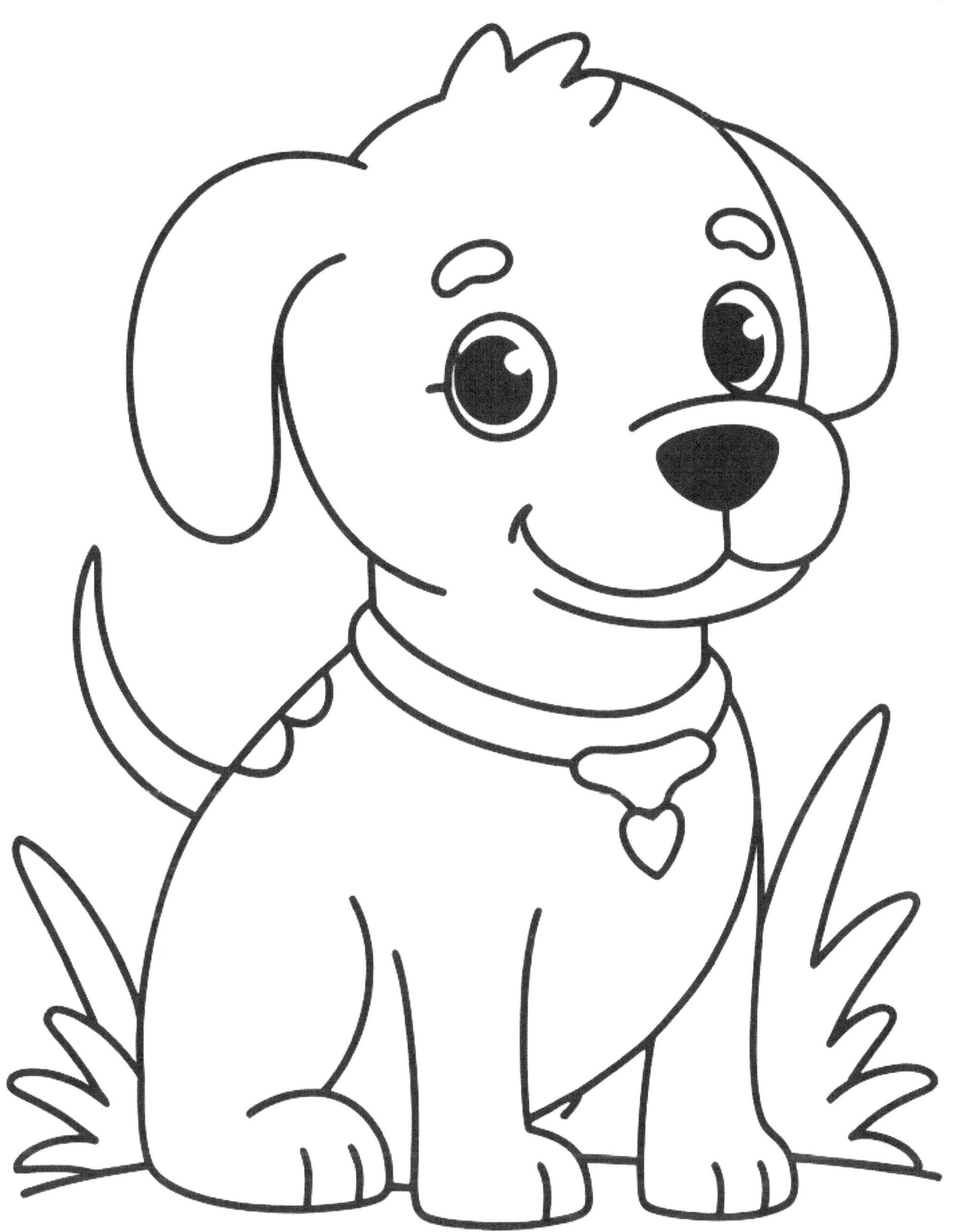

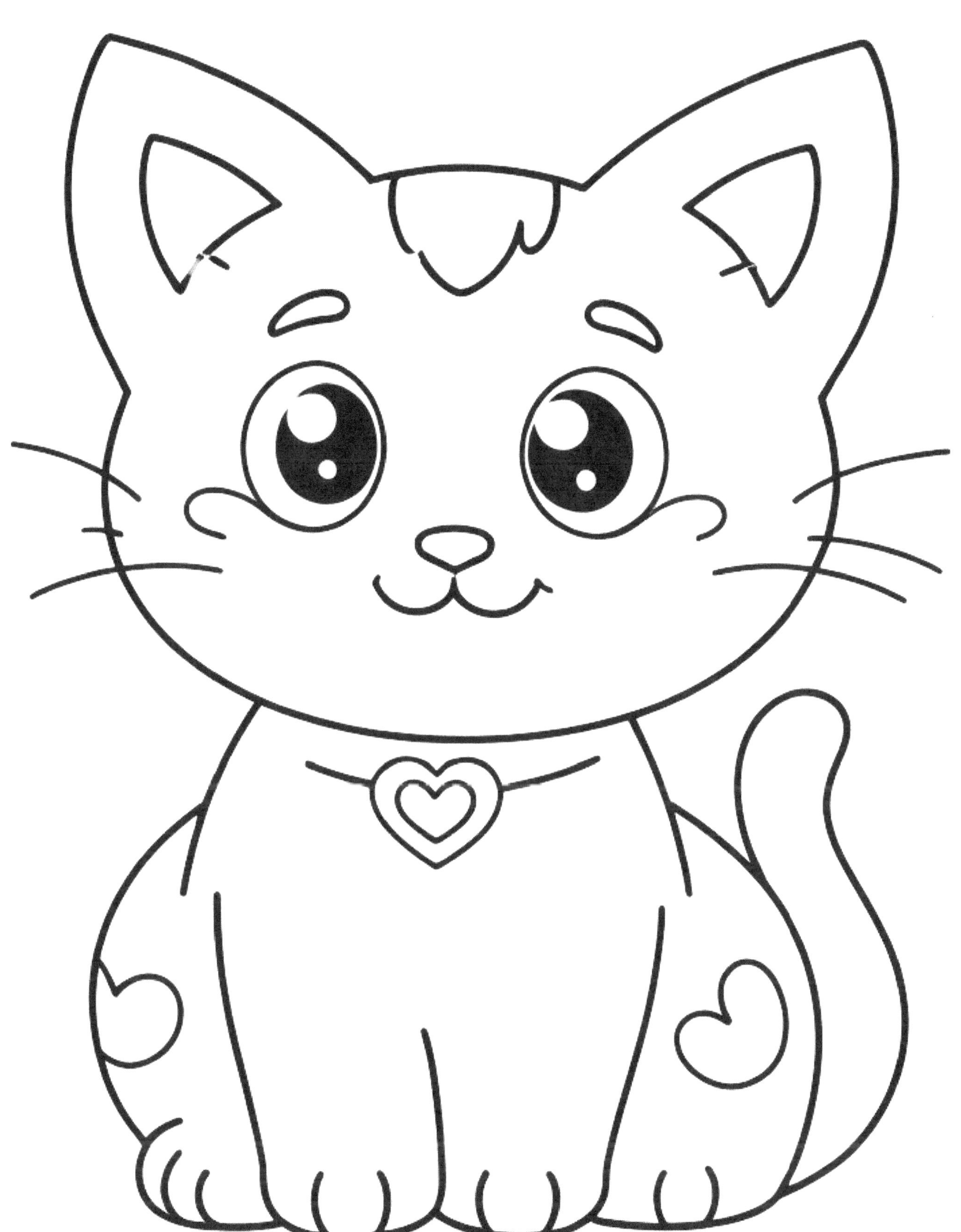

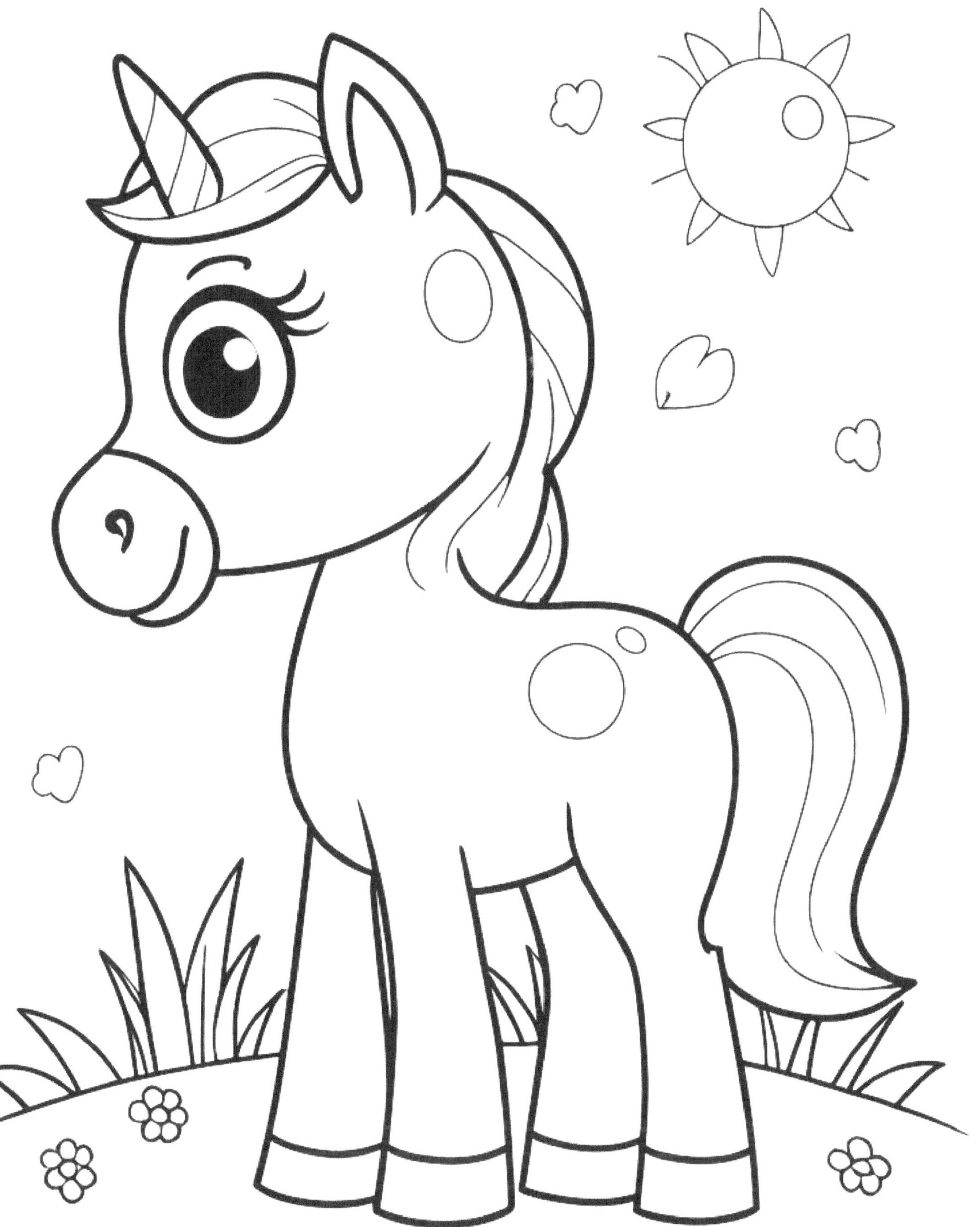

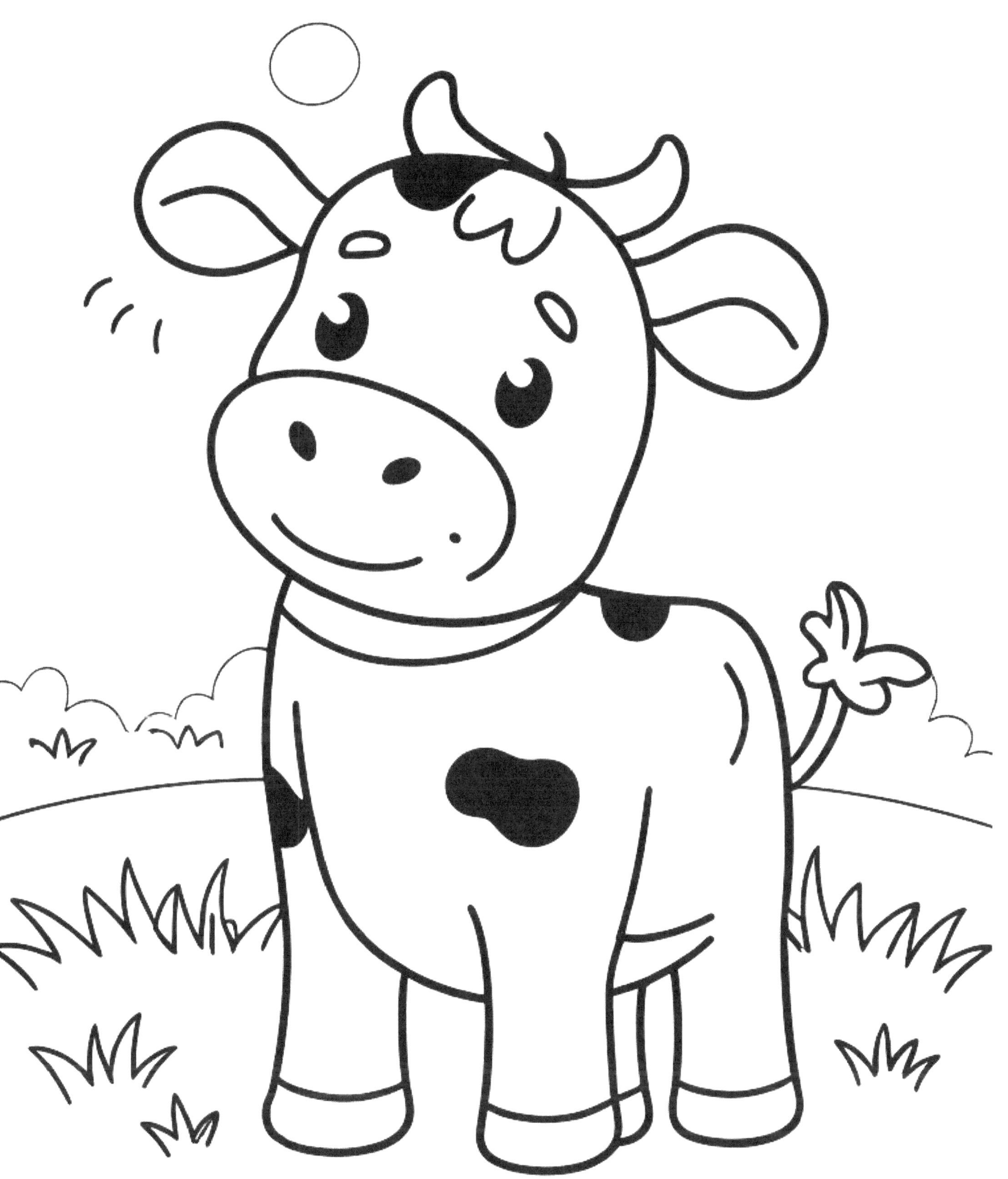

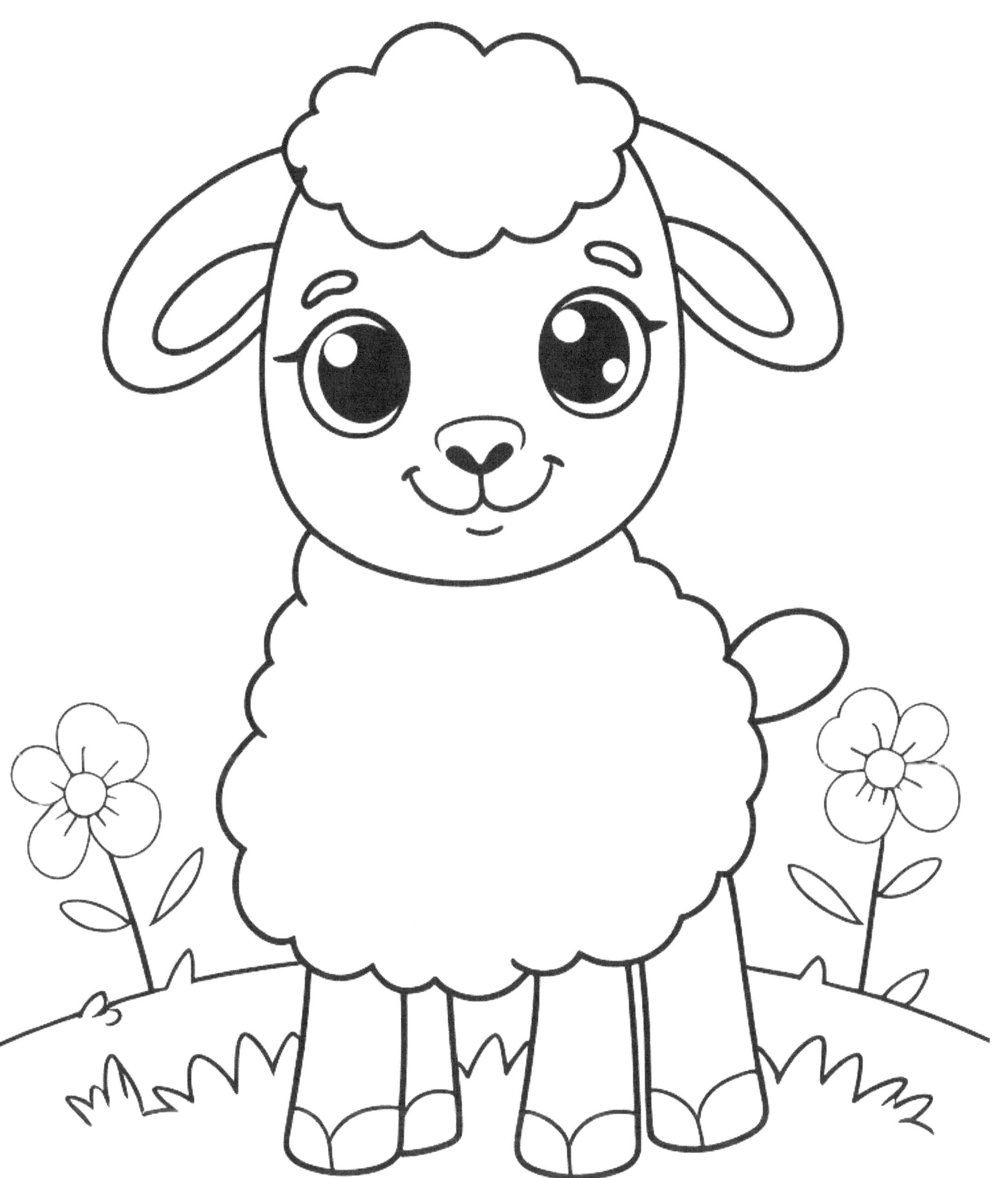

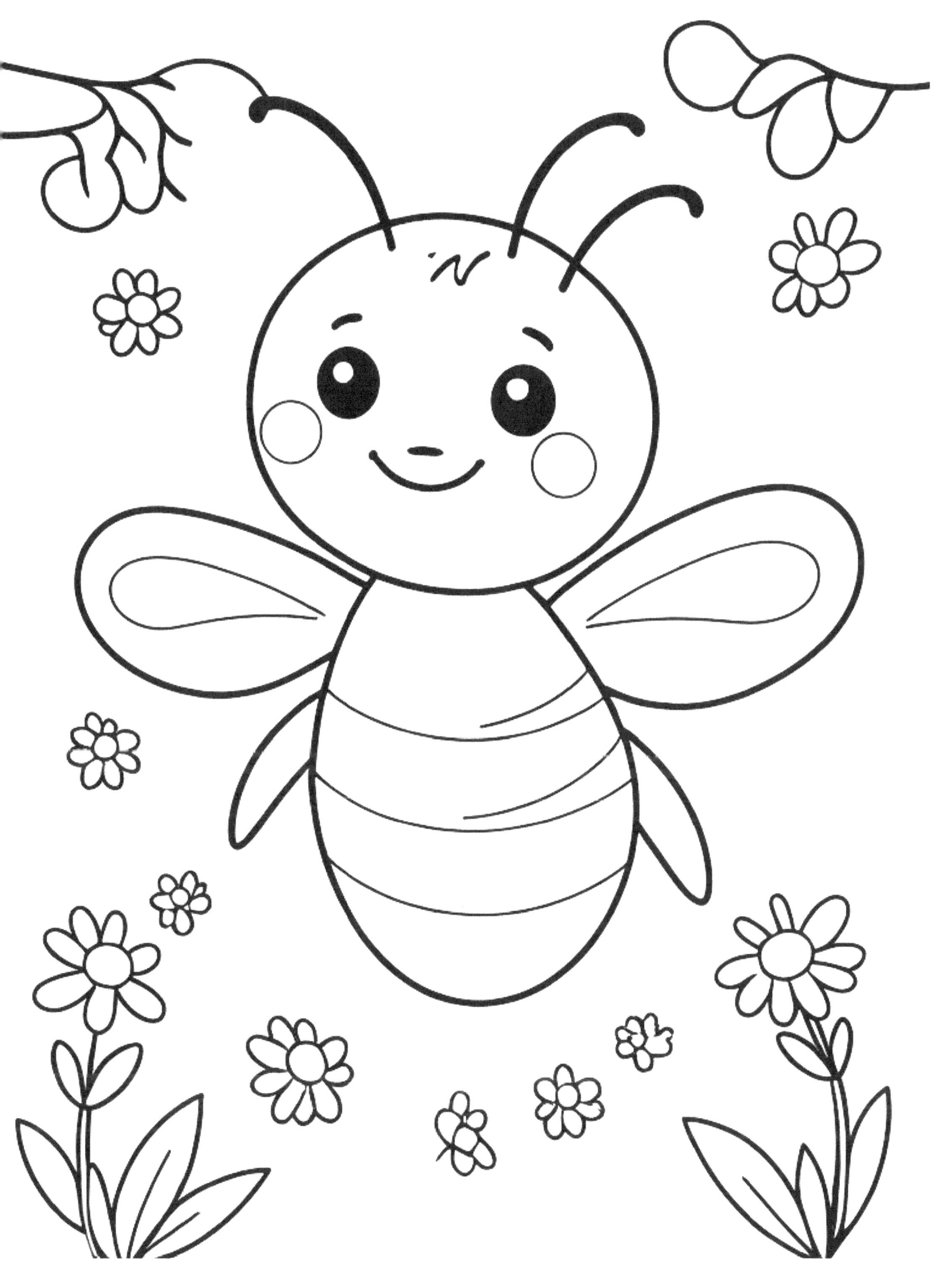

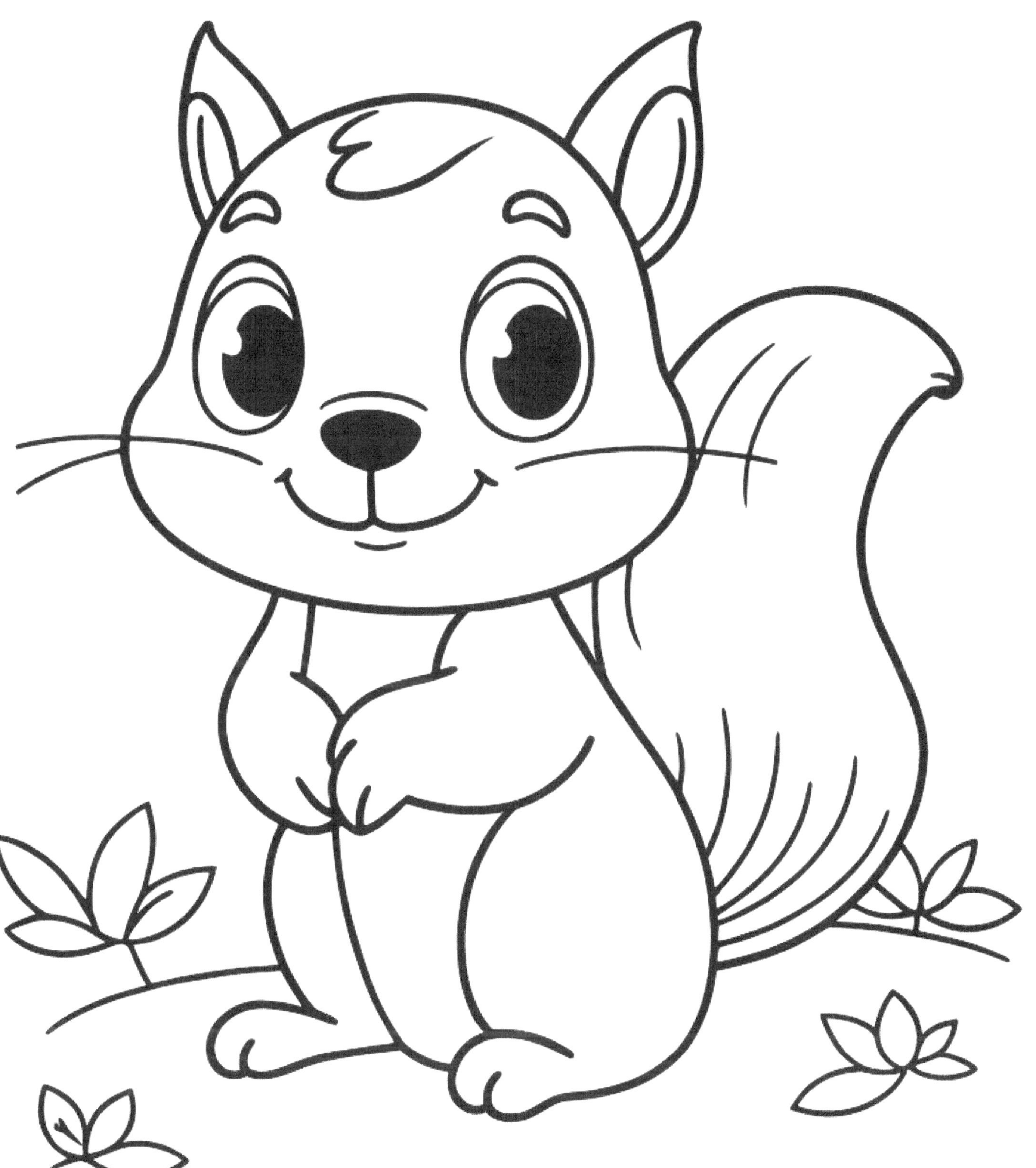

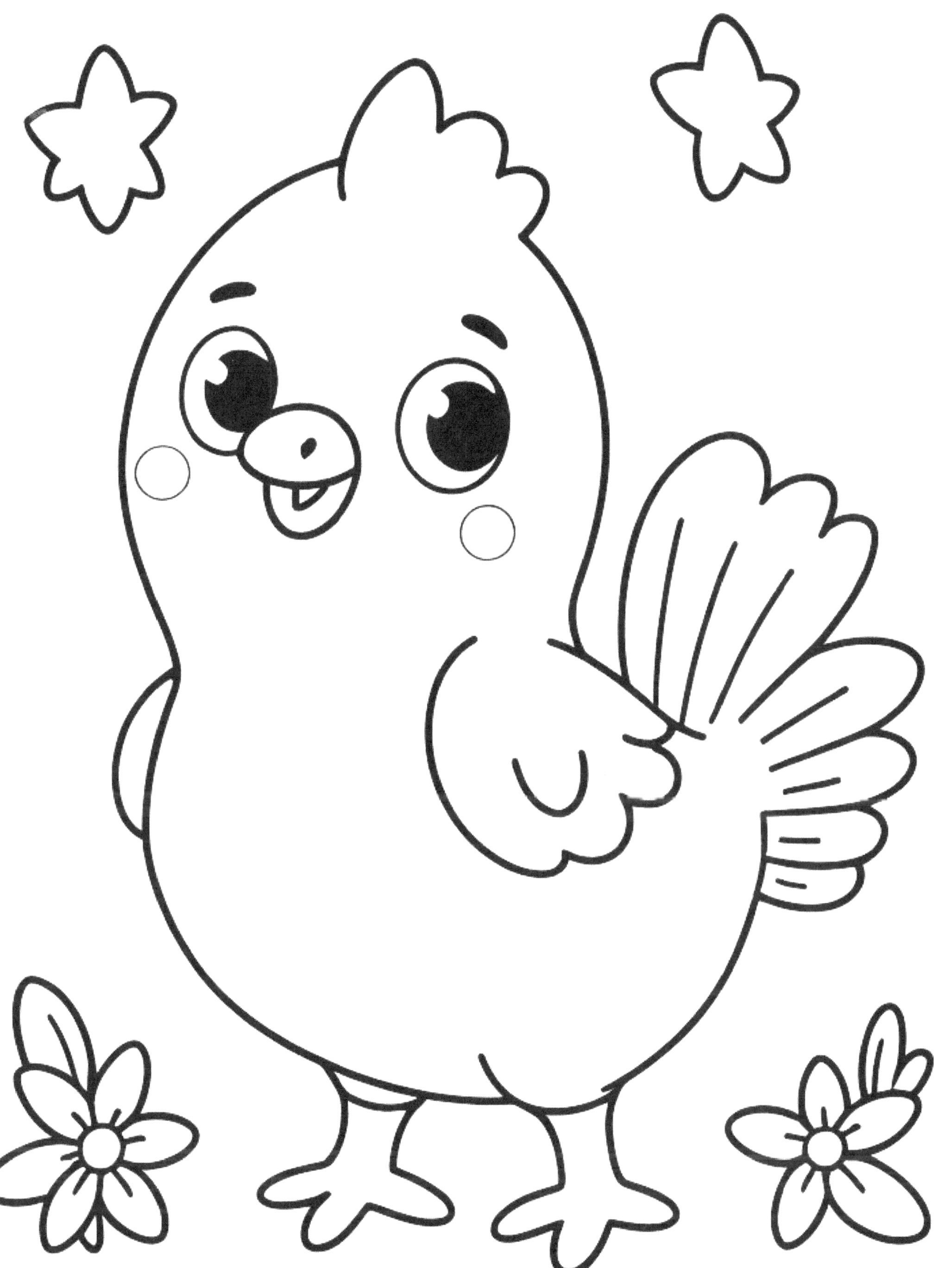

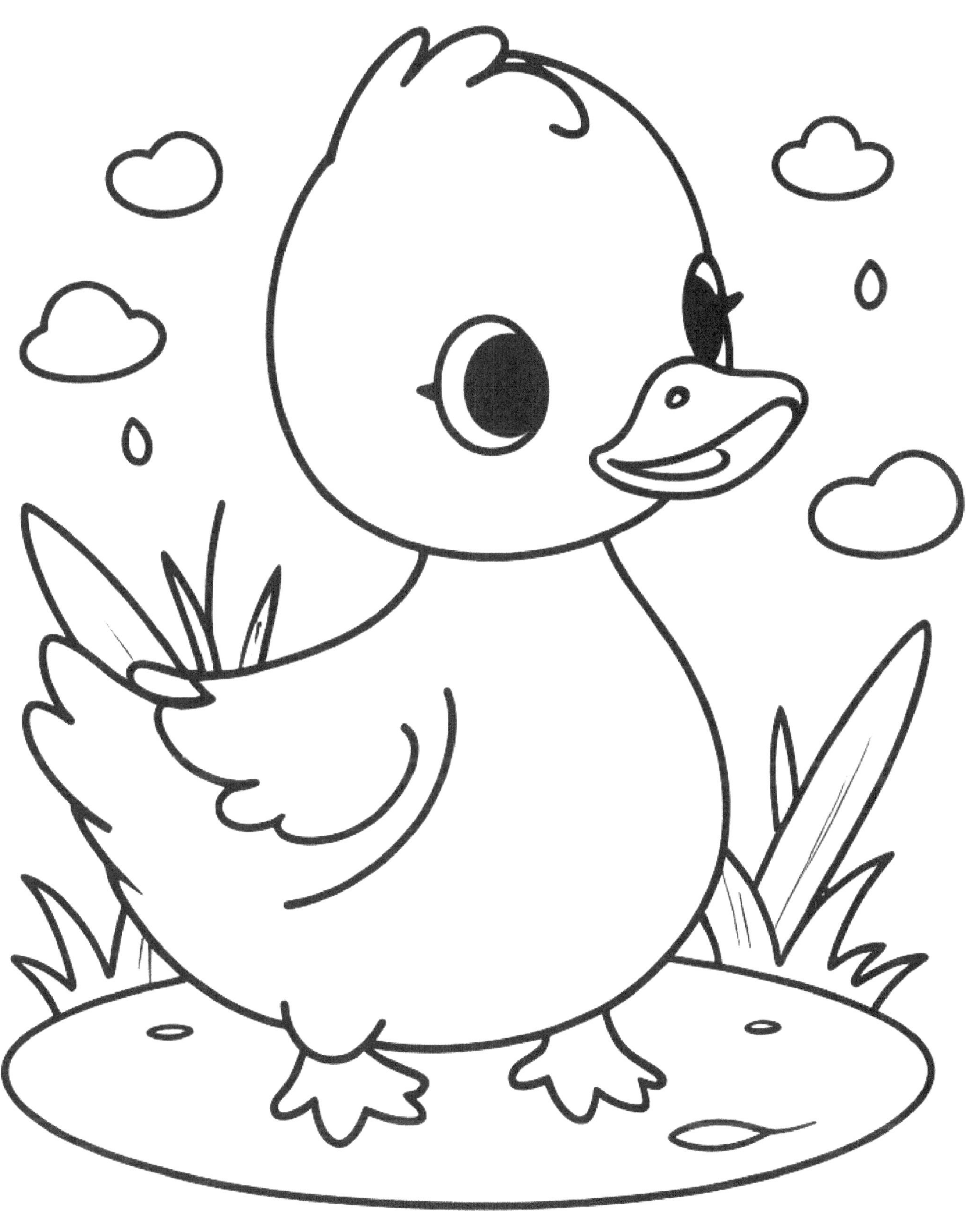

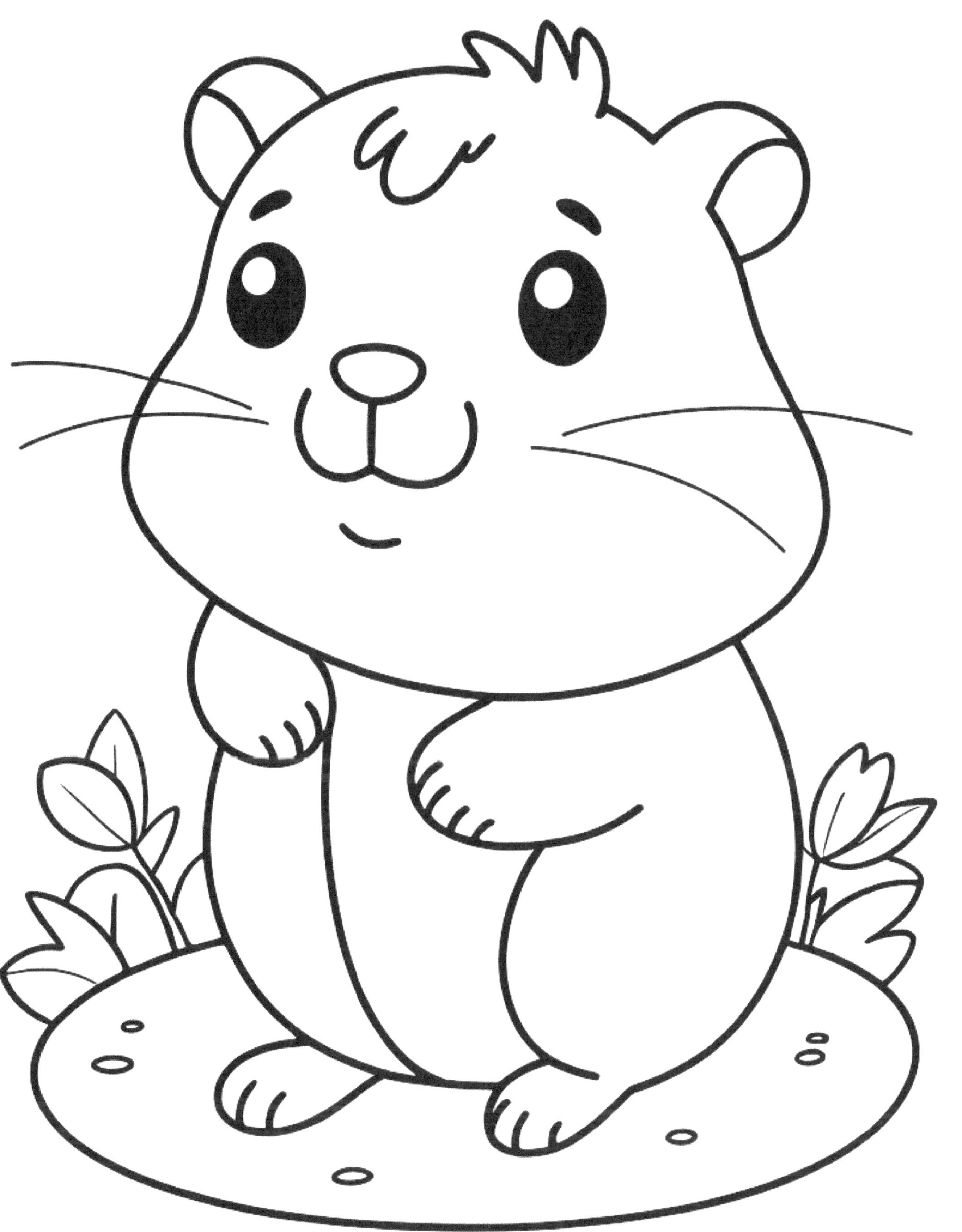

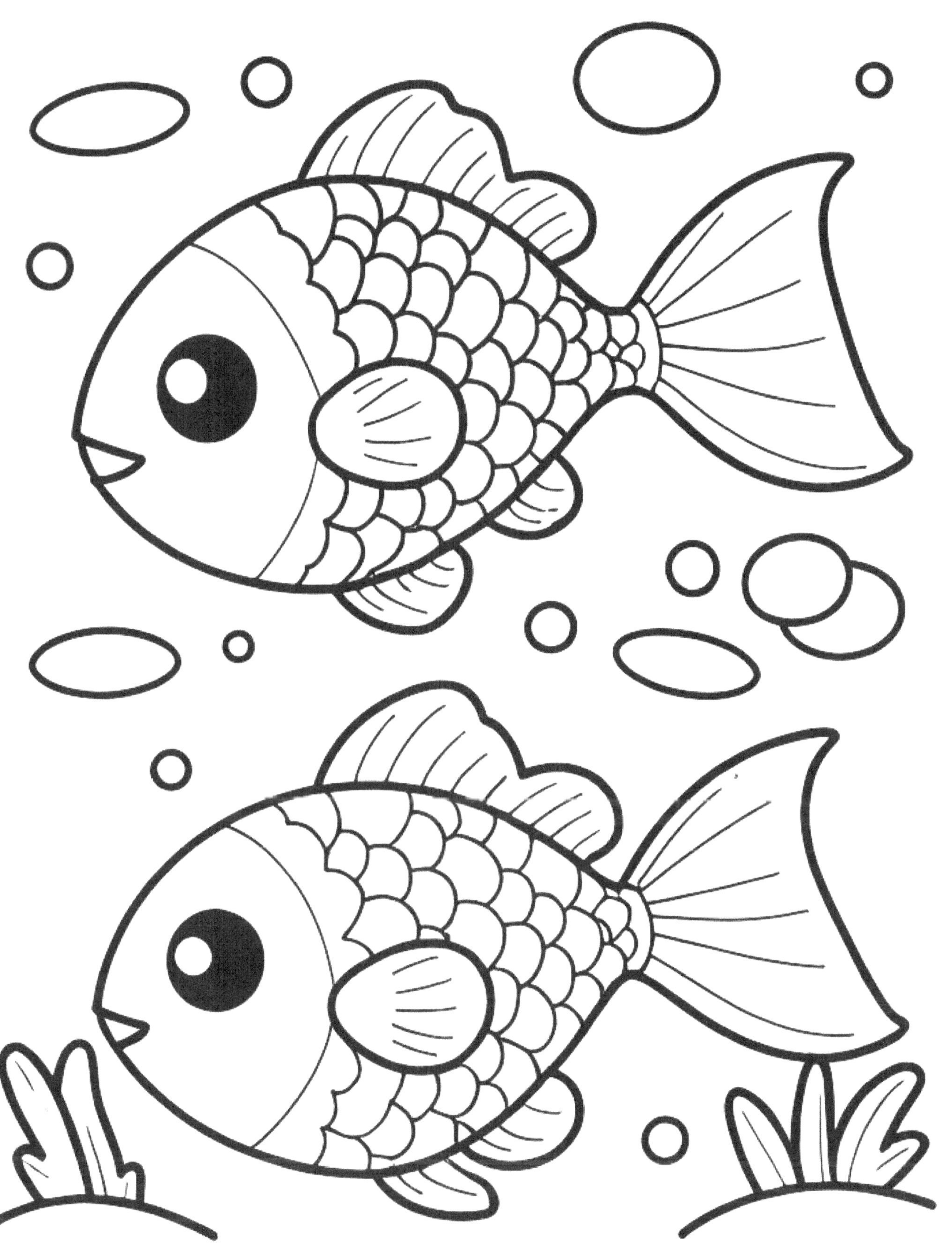

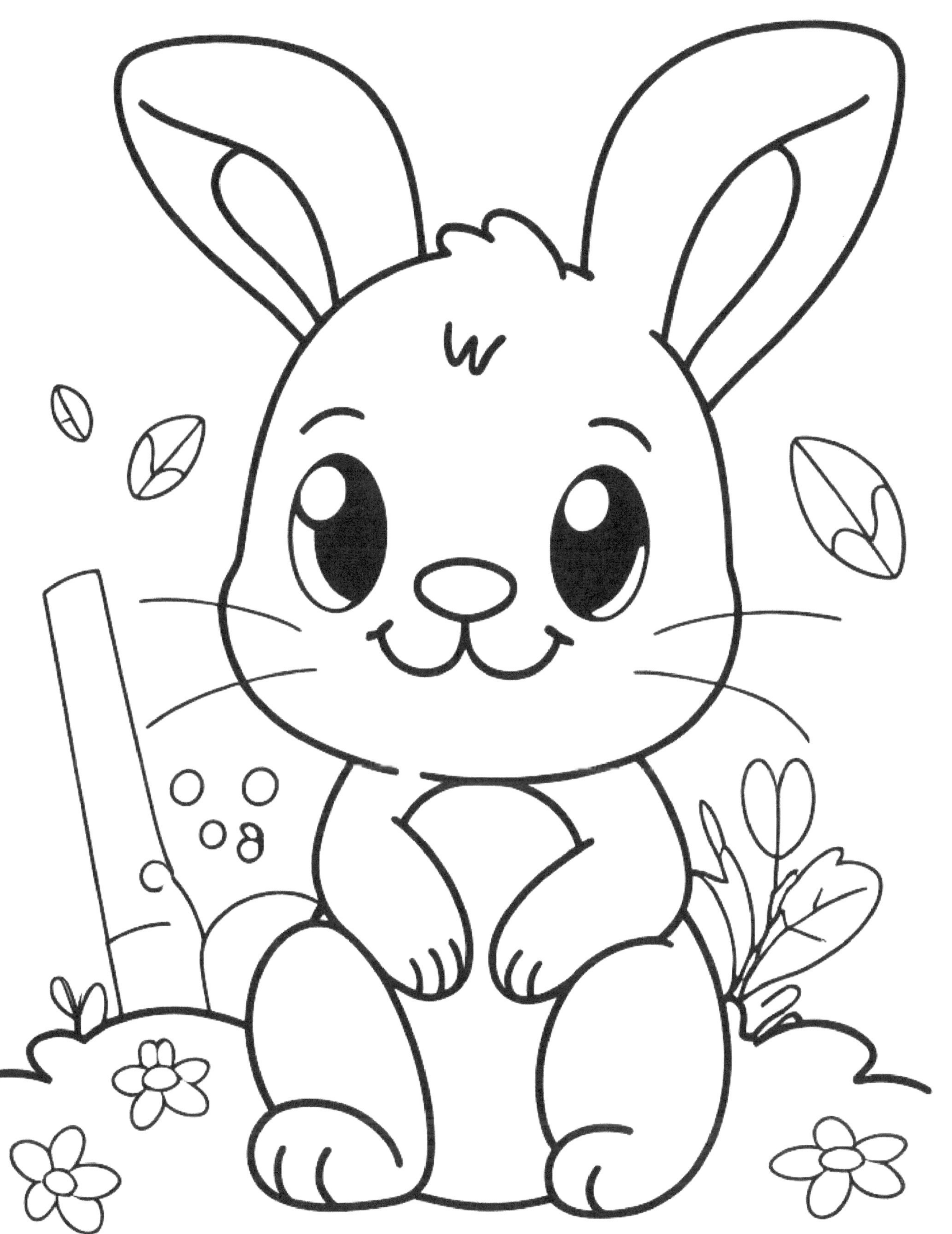

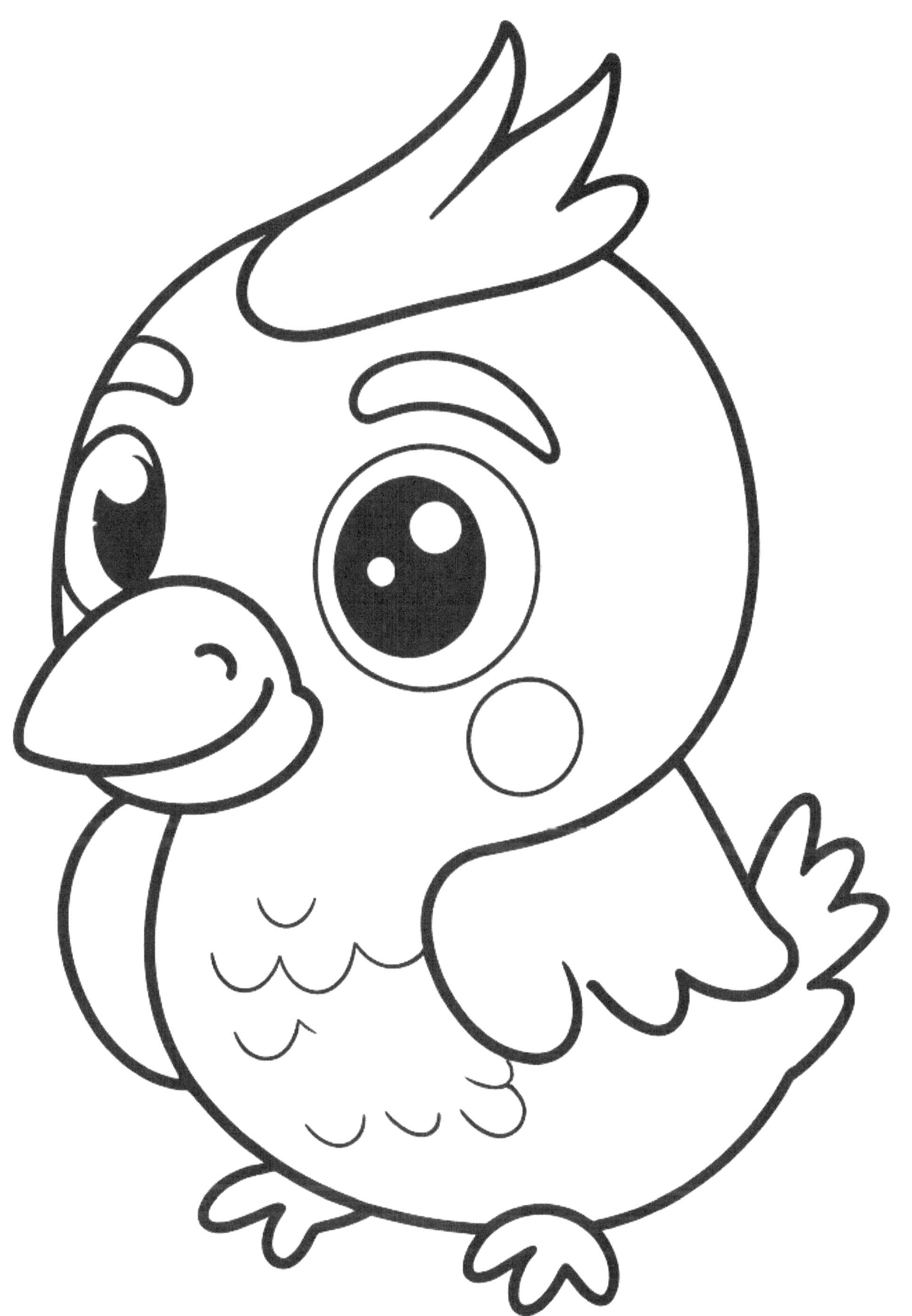

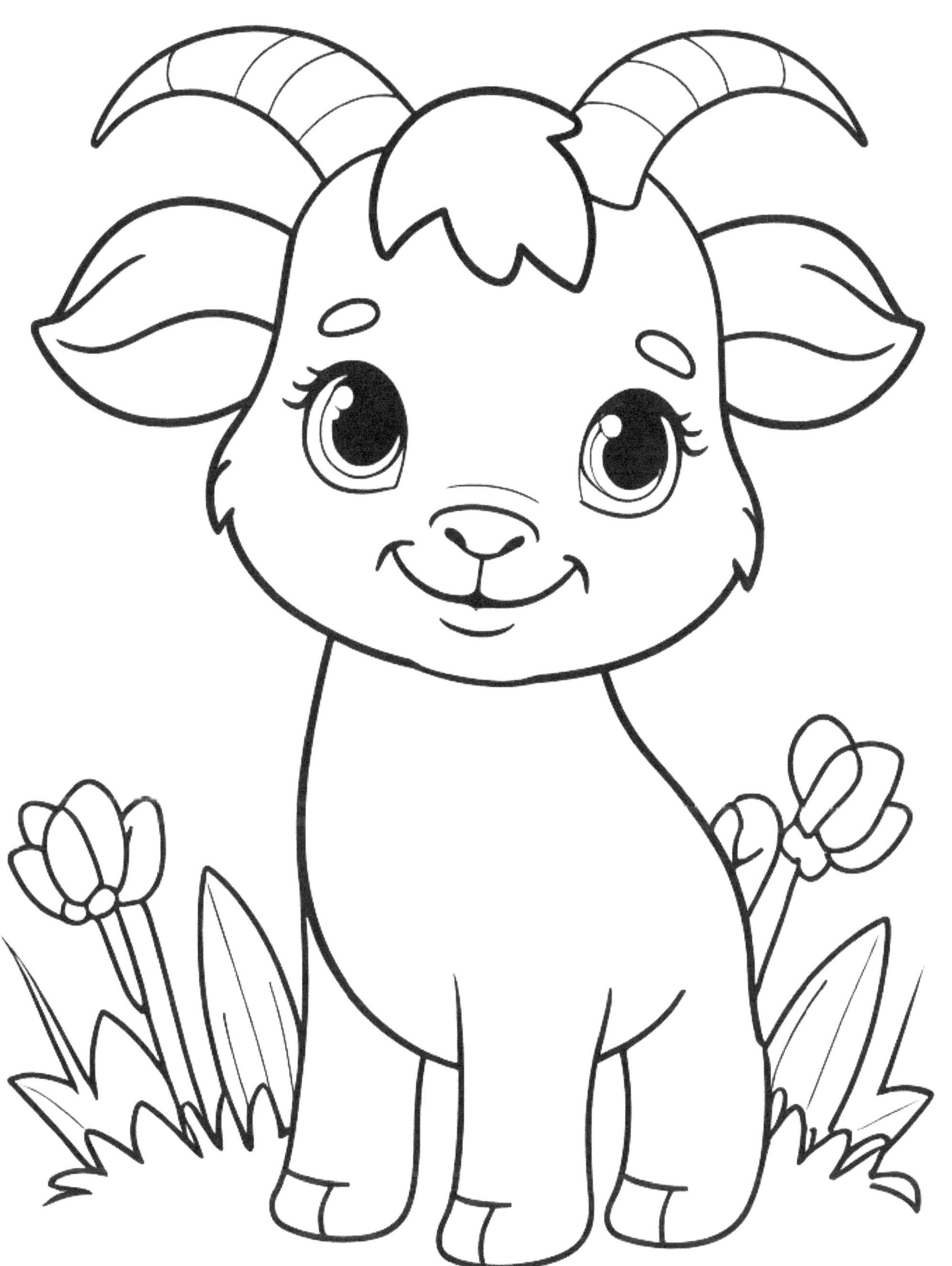